FUSION FLAVORS

FUSION FLAVORS

Creative Mash-Ups for the Modern Kitchen

GIDEON RAYBURN

RWG Publishing

CONTENTS

CHAPTER 1

Introduction to Fusion Flavors

Fusion Flavors is an exciting compilation of dishes that seamlessly marries technical recipes for the advanced or ambitious home cook and entertaining cook's ideas. I led with the cuisine in the title, infusing 12 classes of food with global flavors, techniques, and cultural stylings in ways that could encourage home cooks to expand what is thought of as "possible" in their home kitchens. At the time of writing, while it wasn't difficult to find recipes or dishes liberally called "fusion" in upscale restaurants and cookbooks, it was my observation that popularizing this professional technique for the home cook was minimizing its immense potential.

This led me to the second focus of the book, offering home cooks support to help with advanced level recipes. This was a concern borne out in reviewing feedback from other cookbooks and through direct interviews and surveys conducted with home cooking food bloggers and cook-off participants who consistently aired fear around unpredictable restaurant recipe challenges and frequent outright bias against recipes with challenging ingredients

1

and techniques. The research with contemporary home cooks cul-
minated in data yielding both obvious and quirky guidance as I
developed the content for the introduction to the classes, 28 and 42
menu plans, the recipes, a photo guide, and sidebars I'm delighted to
share in Fusion Flavors. Over the years, that initial focus developed
with the choice of paring down technical content for first-time
cooks in the menu plans and the addition of somewhat adventurous
palates in the 17 and 28 plans.

1.1. Defining Fusion Cuisine

Starting with a definition, fusion cuisine can be classified as a
combination of two or more culinary traditions, achieved through
their selection of ingredients and techniques. Mixed in a single dish,
the ingredients of different cultures' foods can be considered as
composite representations of broader cultural history. The modern
concept of 'fusion cuisine' is understood as 'eclectic fare' or 'mix-
and-match' meals in which a dish combines two distinctive culinary
styles, rather than traditional recipes. It is no longer unusual to
find an unintended blend of traditional ingredients, representing a
global, transient, and dynamically changing traditional style tem-
pered with modern idiosyncrasies. In French cuisine, fusion cuisine
is known as cuisine nouvelle due to the use of new techniques in
dish preparation, whereas the connoisseur of Indian-British fusion
matters does call it 'modern British cuisine'.

1.2. History and Evolution of Fusion Flavors

How is it that different ethnic communities have been able to
intermingle their cherished traditional dishes for centuries, yet the
current popularity of fusion flavors is regarded with such enthusi-
asm yet some degree of suspicion? To answer that question, we
need to consider the basic realities of human nature which have a
profound effect on society. At a basic level, our desire to be together,

to belong, to express warmth, to bond, to comfort, and to establish networks, creates a distinct us-versus-them boundary between people who group together based on some mutual experience or shared characteristic. Such groupings can emerge from a wide variety of factors including language, food, history, art forms, religion, and culture. Social scientists argue that many of these differences are essentially attempts to establish group boundaries.

Although the bold new flavors that ethnic influence produces can seem quite modern, the creative use of diverse ingredients is actually an age-old approach. Virtually every group of immigrants in America's young history brought culinary practices that were a fusion of various components. In fact, many traditional dishes emerged where the cuisine of different groups rubbed against one another. As we examine the history of fusion flavors, we'll see repeatedly how they flourished at the border between two culinary traditions. Not unexpectedly, such culinary hybridization and flair for bold new flavors are hallmarks of America's global kitchens.

CHAPTER 2

The Art of Flavor Pairing

Throughout the book, you will find explanations for these pairings with backstories that result in extraordinary flavor material. And there are the stories that show the passion of passionate coming together in contemporary and classic fare, featuring exciting ingredients and creative techniques in delicious dishes. They are mash-ups representing the best flavors of the several diverse cultures as globetrotting chefs break the boundaries. Join the journey, have close your eyes, and savor our delicious trip through the history of flavors on the tongue.

Dare to be different. Get out of your flavor rut and turn off that autopilot. Everyday meals can be interesting and contribute to lively mealtime conversation. We are today's explorers, setting sail on the spice route or opening wide the New World pantry. To send our foods on new ventures, think in terms of pairings and mash-ups. Create a bridge that spans the continents, between their traditions and ancient culinary wisdom, and our lives here and now. To create those bridges, look to the past for inspiration. Think about what makes classic Belgian mussels, Greek yogurt and cucumber, and Middle Eastern lemon-flavored cookies go together. Why sushi chefs offer pickled ginger or brewers serve pretzels with beer. Are they overrated traditions, or could their reasons be held dear as you set sail on the Fusion Flavor Flavors Fleet?

2.1. Understanding Flavor Profiles

The flavor profile of an herb or spice is a sum of its flavor parts as well. Each of our more commonly used culinary herbs – basil, coriander, cilantro, tarragon, mint, parsley, dill, thyme, and chervil - are predominantly single-note flavors, although generally reflecting a green or earthy sour taste. Rosemary and oregano have singularities such as camphor and bitterness, while caraway and cardamom are sweet undertoned, cinnamon and cloves naturally sweet, and fennel or cumin more spicy or otherwise well-rounded. There are sweeter herbs and spices like cinnamon, cloves, and fennel, and some more spicy, such as cayenne or scotch bonnet peppers. And you could throw together ginger, saffron, or vanilla. The last three are the most polarizing in that they are both distinct and memorable, and when paired together, tend to produce an unstable or volatile overall flavor that can be intoxicating to some and displeasing to others.

Each ingredient used for a dish has a flavor profile - a combination of the five sensations: sweet, sour, salty, bitter, and umami. Many cooks interpret this to be a way of understanding different tastes, as discovered during the act of eating, but the concept of flavor profile also can help you select flavors to use in a recipe creation. A squirt of ketchup in a soup can add sweetness, a drizzle of vinegar can add sour flavor, soy sauce adds saltiness, radicchio provides bitterness, and Dijon mustard contributes savory umami.

2.2. Balancing Sweet, Sour, Salty, Bitter, and Umami

Sweet, sour, salty, umami, and bitter create transformative strength within food, enrich the enjoyment factor, and comfort the soul. Treat these balancing, aerobic groceries with the respect they deserve or prepare for mealtime mediocrity. Enhance their flavors through a merging of fresh, local, in-season ingredients, proper cooking, and serving techniques, and watch all the stars fall into line and shine. Experience how simple yet sublime it is when a bowl of ribollita brings cheer on a nipping winter day, savor ravioli stuffed with saffron - Pecorino Romano - Parmigiano Reggiano brown butter, note the down-to-earth comfort a bowl of fish flops fond reverence for raw Alaskan halibut ceviche. As with fashion, some foods burst onto the world stage with flair, while others emerge with soundly practical no-nonsense deliciousness. All beg our admiration.

I've finally arrived at the heart of the matter - balancing the elements of God, Nature, the forces of the universe: sweet, sour, salty, bitter, and umami. In Sanskrit, they are referred to as 'rasas'. Together, they unite to give a dish a full, rounded, balanced rasa. Balance these five in a dish and magic happens. The number five is woven through seasons, senses, temperatures, uncooked and cooked foods, and daily routines. We agree with the food scientist Harold McGee, creator of the concept of rasa, and that these five rasas cover all tastes and textures. Seasonal ingredients spin new flavors and textures with a sparkle of color every three months. Muster a 'do it yourself' attitude, a dash of equilibrium, light speed internet access, tips from brilliant chefs, and keep abreast of experimental, seasonal food photography, lean hard on the network of food aficionados, and reinvent dinner.

CHAPTER 3

Techniques for Successful Fusion Cooking

Technique 1. Understand your ingredients: Understanding your ingredients is an essential aspect of successful cooks, yet you should try to understand your ingredients in atypical method as fusion chefs. The instances listed in the following paragraphs will enlarge your knowledge of some peculiarly haute ingredients, conventional and considered normal. However, know that haute cuisine often has humble provenance. The following paragraphs list both lesser-known and now-popular exotic ingredients - are recommended to you for short references. These can easily elevate your food.

In any ongoing creative endeavor as unbound as fusion cuisine, successful results are infinitely varied and measurable in only the most subjective ways. Conversing with a diner nostalgic for a long-gone classic preparation, such as a trendy, drugstore-style chicken teriyaki with crispy soba noodles, manifests instant kudos for the chef as a sympathetic ear - an understanding of the love of nostalgia. Or delighting a diner with a thrilling and likeable gamble in innovative ingredients, such as Sautéed Mayoonyi™ (with chili peppers and a cup of high-end sour cream), earns appreciation for wit and daring. But the following techniques will help guarantee that your most inventive fusion culinary attempts will be successful on a broader and more technical basis, combining food history, universally accepted flavor profiles, and the variety of global traditions better than an uptowner's palate could hope.

3.1. Blending Cooking Methods

Braising followed by baking or broiling can be used to transform plain, shredded leftover chicken or turkey into a seasoned, herb-speckled, and spiked chicken or turkey salad. As a finishing technique, broiling and baking differ in their distance from the heat source; broiling is close, fast, and delivers a direct blast of energy; baking is indirect and uses a consistent and steady heat. After a brief grill, a quick sauté, or a long braise, the oven is often the ideal tool to slow-cook, roast, or bake hearty and sturdy pasta and grain dishes that are savored for their heady aroma, earthy flavors, and nurturing warmth.

Braising, broiling, baking, grilling, or frying are each stand-alone cooking methods that produce very different and distinct textures, flavors, and characteristics. Mixing and matching these methods is a great way to enhance the final dish by layering diverse flavors, textures, and nutrients—saving time and reducing energy consumption to boot. Many dishes follow an actual "two-step" roadmap that starts with braising and then ends with grilling. Braising fish or chicken in a flavor-packed liquid gently cooks the protein and infuses it with layers of moist and juicy flavors. Grilling finishes the dish with smoky and charred flavor notes.

3.2. Incorporating Ingredients from Different Cultures

Just as the maturation of beer, cheese, and wine, increase in regional production, and the globalization of trade have broadened palates worldwide, the availability of ingredients from other continents in local supermarkets means that most of us are able to incorporate fusion flavors into the food we cook at home. Twenty years ago, finding cavolo nero, simple garlic, or good olive oil would have required a trip to a specialist deli, especially if you lived outside inner-city London. But the world has changed and is a smaller place. Only the most insular will not have tasted mezze, tapas, dim sum, or a sandwich in the last fortnight. Sushi is as easy to come by as a BBC recipe for a ploughman's meal. Only in Britain is a cup of sweet milky coffee not part of a daily routine, downed with a portion of sweet, doughy wheat-based toast for breakfast. The immigration of people and food has brought deliciousness to a wider audience.

We all eat food from other cultures. Whether we are eating at an authentic ethnic restaurant or consuming mass-produced standardized food like chicken fingers, sushi, or spaghetti, our tastes today are more varied and diverse. In my last book, "The Geometry of Pasta," Caz Hildebrand and I visited the origins of pasta shapes and their traditional Italian sauces. Now, in "Fusion Flavours," I am looking at how, in a wider context, using influences from one cuisine to flavor another means we can enjoy the best of global tucker at home. As we become more sophisticated food consumers, it is not only commercial takeaways run by national culinary ambassadors which use ingredients from different places.

CHAPTER 4

Mediterranean-Inspired Fusions

To both approximate these diets and maintain the integrity of these foods, the foundation of Mediterranean cooking – the olive oil, garlic, and tomato – are used throughout the sections each time a merging takes place. To add the full and wonderful flavors of the Mediterranean, include throughout your cooking repertoire the produce, spices, and cheese you'll encounter in the recipes and also included are these ingredients.

Mediterranean cuisine, with its emphasis on grains, roasted meats and vegetables, small flavorful appetizers, and rustic breads, offers such great possibilities for food fusion. Here's how you can go about creating similar fusions in your own kitchen, either using these recipes as a template or designing your own from your knowledge of the cuisine. A word of caution: traditional Mediterranean diets, such as that of Greece or Southern Italy, are renowned for their brilliant health effects and delicious simplicity.

4.1. Greek-Mexican Fusion

Grilled gyro pork stuffed into soft pepper tortillas and topped with chunky green pineapple salsa and Greek guacamole (Yes, guacamole! Mexican appetizer, Greek seasonings!)

In central Mexico, street stalls offer a whole pig roasted al pastor, thickly sliced, and stuffed into a fist-sized corn tortilla with slices of fresh pineapple and a chunky green pineapple salsa. Here, the meat is first seared, then roasted a la manera griega (the Greek way). The dish has Mexican al pastor and Greek gyro in its genes.

How do you blend Greek and Mexican flavors successfully? You look for the compatible elements of both culinary traditions to create a dish that can hold its head high in either company. That means you have to include the sunny, smoky flavors of Greek cooking and the zesty, vivid ones of Mexico.

4.2. Italian-Indian Fusion

Italian-Indian Tomato Onion Chicken - 4 pieces of chicken - Salt - Avocado oil - 1 medium red onion, peeled, halved, and sliced into half-moon slivers - 4 cloves garlic, peeled and smashed - 1 inch ginger, peeled and grated - 1/2 teaspoon cumin seeds - 1/2 teaspoon ground coriander - 1/4-1/2 teaspoon cayenne pepper - 1/2 teaspoon garam masala - 1/2 teaspoon turmeric - 1/2 teaspoon salt - 1 cup diced tomatoes, fresh or canned, drained of extra liquid

Italian-Indian? You're probably scratching your head about now, but I guarantee this is going to knock your socks off. It's proof once again that onions and tomatoes can cross cultural lines with abandon. This dish combines a classic tomato and onion sauce with Indian spices for a rich, deep flavor. The hardest part of this recipe is managing not to nibble the finished chicken before you're ready to eat. The chicken pieces are equally at home resting at the bottom of hot, fragrant sauce as they are the star of a multi-ethnic potluck.

Braise the bird in keto-friendly chicken broth or stock for a tasty companion side dish.

CHAPTER 5

Asian Fusion Creations

In Szechuan Chicken Thirty-Minute Casserole, microwaving the dish saves one step by eliminating the need to precook the chicken and cook the vegetables. Microwave cooking saves a bit of cooking time in Chicken and Green Onion Noodles. Soy sauces layered with wasabi deliver a fresh dipping sauce for Grilled Tofu Skewers. Chinese tea dances with fish sauce, soy, cinnamon, orange, ginger, garlic, and serrano in Five-Spice Oyster Casserole, recorded in Canadian Grandmaster Kim's Lemon-Lime Cookbook. Dory or whitefish pieces join oyster mushrooms in the broth to create an elegant fish soup. Stir-frying has claimed such a place in Western cuisine that many home cooks have added woks and mandolins to their kitchen arsenal. With Thirteen Stir-Fry Vegetable Salad, the cuisine seems almost simplistic. The side salad partners well with garlic and ginger stir or deep-fried chicken served in wraps. Pork, garlic and ginger also appear in layered wonton parcels with fennel and coriander. Authentic Fried Squid rings wear an Asian recipe and with lite soy with thai or sweet chili might bring a plate of seafood delicacies to the dinner table. Where else might Ponzu Sauce and Ginger Marinade end up on a salad or savoury dessert? under the cooking category, the section devoted to beverage brewing may be a record of barley water or vegetarian soup, but it almost assuredly winds up under hot and pungent titles of Cumin Tea or Chicken and Cashews. The spicy broth soothes the winter chills while delighting the tastebuds with additional warmth.

Asian cuisines offer a seemingly endless menu of flavors. If you've never worked with fermented black beans, you're missing out on a flavor-packed ingredient that can bind your stir-fry or rice dish with extreme gusto. In Cast-Iron Japanese-Style Beef, a steak is marinated in sake, soy, and mirin for deep, rich flavor. This recipe includes a bonus of steaming the beef, allowing for minimal cooking time. Free radicals are suggested to be a cause of aging, but antioxidant Vitamins E and C are in abundance in Spinach with Fermented Black Beans. Gingered Fruit Salad, Sweet-and-Sour Asian Tofu Salad, New England Crab Rangoon Salad, and Beef and Blue Salad all provide a hint of Asian in tossed salads. Dressing elements such as soy sauce, rice or balsamic vinegar, ginger, and toasted sesame oil wore dual hats. In Asian Carrot Soup, star anise is a star anise offering both flavor infusion and garnish speculation. The annual festival celebrated in Japan at the time of blooming sakura inspired sweet Cherry Fizz Drinks and National Cherry Festival's Turkey Sushi Assortment.

5.1. Japanese-Peruvian Fusion

As Japanese laborers and their families became residents and citizens, the populations co-mingled and began, usually through their cooking, to mix two culinary traditions. By the end of the twentieth century, Japanese-Peruvian fusion had coalesced into a style recognized throughout the world. Today, Nikkei (a modified form of the polite word for "Japanese") cuisine brings fresh fish, copious lemons and limes, seaweed, soy sauce, rice vinegar, ginger, red pepper, mirin (sweet rice cooking wine), and other Japanese cooking flavors into the Peruvian kitchen and, often, onto the Peruvian grill. Some people claim that Peru is home to the first pure fusion cuisine, richer and more exalted than any other, because of the bonding of traditional cuisines from Peru, Spain, Africa, China, Japan, Italy, and Arabia, forged by political and social upheavals.

Lima, Peru, is a notoriously impossible city located high along the Pacific side of South America. In Lima, a fusion cuisine created by immigrant Japanese workers and their children has caught the gastronomic world's attention. Japanese-Peruvian fusion became a surprising crossover success. Japanese immigrant workers came to the Lima region to work on sugar plantations, starting around 1899 and continuing through World War I and beyond. The Japanese workers brought their cooking techniques and also grew familiar crops such as sweet potatoes.

5.2. Korean-Texan Fusion

Fusion stirs people's imaginations and often gets more than just a passing glance. These delicious Korean/Texan tacos promise to intrigue and delight. The very moist beef - which comes courtesy of a Korean-style marinade and a trip to the beloved smoker - gets a layer of bitter-chocolatey mole and creamy avocado. The Korean-Texan combo is a creative mashup, and the fusion promises to intrigue and delight.

Texas barbecue is legendary. It's also completely out of context in Korean cooking. But as I always say, "When it tastes good, it tastes good." So I headed to Korean Taco barbecue truck pioneer Roy Choi's best buddy Alice McGurke for some advice and arrived confident at this combination. A tangy Korean-style marinade and a trip to the beloved smoker added an incredibly juicy layer of flavor to something already wonderful. These tacos also get a layer of deep, dark bitter chocolatey mole to drive home the flavor. Set it all into a soft griddled corn tortilla and top with your favorite condiments. Then chow down!

CHAPTER 6

Exploring Fusion Desserts

The two recipes in this section integrate fruit, spices, and sauces with components and baking styles from across the globe. Each of these recipes would end an exotic dinner party spectacularly, proving conclusively that prepared in the right mixture, two can become one. Fusion fondants are warm with Asian spices, a perfect compliment for the Summer fruit compots with a hint of chili. The base recipe for the fondant is similar to molten or non-setting chocolate cakes that have been popular since the early nineties, a perfect treat for chocolate lovers everywhere. Although these types of cakes are made to have soft centers, or 'lava', the fondants are a little different - mainly because they are so much more difficult to bake.

Merging the best of sweet from two unquestionable stars of the dessert pantheon allows you, the creative genius, to come up with desserts that are unusual, sophisticated, and truly memorable. Unexpected flavor combinations take on an even greater dimension in a dessert: evidence of the funky and exotic can be balanced and rounded by an exquisite finish, rendering the final bite of the meal more than a mere sugar rush. Lighter flavors such as fruits, spices, and nuts are automatically culprits for being pushed into the spotlight. To this, you can add a myriad of dessert suggestions, inspired from the fusion kitchen, where Californian meets South American, Mediterranean shakes hand with the Far East, and home taste Japanese satisfaction.

6.1. French-Japanese Pastry Mash-Ups

French cuisine emphasizes starting with the top-quality ingredient to make few ingredients shine their best with nothing to hide behind. Japanese philosophy on showcasing the ingredients is similar. Both origins seem to arise when people at a time of peace and prosperity decided to simply enjoy the best that life has to offer. In this collection, I choose to focus on Japanese and French mash-ups. However, the urge to blend what is best in all cooking traditions is shared by so many chefs and home bakers. I hope that this chapter can also inspire you to discover and explore the beautiful collision at the intersection of the world's exceptional baking heritage.

Many of the best desserts and pastries of the world mix and meld influences from all over the globe. A world without Russian Napoleon cake, Danish pastries, and croissants would be unthinkable. So for the next three recipes, I set out to develop French-Japanese pastry mash-ups that would blend the best of these two glorious traditions, and could be enjoyed at any time of the day. Enter the matcha crème caramel with genoise cake, black sesame madeleines, and yuzu ginger blueberry crème mousseline tart. In each recipe, I deliberately blend the two culinary styles and attempt to marry the best of both worlds to taste and look as if neither ever existed on its own. While creating these recipes, I found that while these fusion recipes seem to draw from opposite ends of the culinary spectrum, their underlying principles have much in common.

6.2. Mexican-Chinese Sweet Treats

Cool the pecans on the sheet for at least 20 minutes. Use a fork to separate any remaining clumps and enjoy immediately.

Instructions: Preheat the oven to 325°F (165°C). Heat a non-stick skillet over medium-high heat. Add the oil and sugar, and cook, swirling every 20 to 30 seconds, for about 1 minute, until golden and bubbly. Add the egg white to the skillet and swirl for about 1 minute, until thick and fluffy. Add the pinenuts (if using) and stir until the sugar caramelizes and the pine nuts are golden. Scrape the mixture into a large heatproof bowl. In a small saucepan, lightly whisk together the miso and agave over medium heat. Add the garlic, ginger, cayenne, and cinnamon and bring the mixture to a simmer. Continue to knead and stir the miso paste constantly for about 2 minutes, until it loosens and has homogenized to a loose paste. Remove the miso mixture from the heat and scrape it into the bowl with the caramel. Swirl the pecans in the bowl with the miso mixture, stirring firmly to coat the nuts evenly; work quickly, as the miso glaze will harden as it cools. Turn the glazed nuts out onto a rimmed baking sheet and separate any clusters. Roast, shaking the sheet or stirring the nuts every 2 to 3 minutes, for 5 to 7 minutes, until glossy, fragrant, and the sugar has crisped.

Do not use the liquid type of miso for this recipe; it is too salty and can be overwhelming when reduced. Pecans, like all nuts, are high in oils that can go rancid. To maximize freshness, I stock up on nuts and freeze them in heavy-duty ziplock bags in manageable portions.

Ingredients: 2 tablespoons (30 ml) mild vegetable oil, such as grapeseed ⅓ cup (2.6 oz./75 g) granulated sugar 1 large egg white 2 tablespoons pinenuts (optional) 2 tablespoons (25 g) white miso 1 teaspoon agave nectar 2 large garlic cloves 1 teaspoon (3 g) minced fresh ginger ½ teaspoon cayenne (pack enough oomph for some heat, but not so much that they are spicy) Scant ¼ teaspoon ground cinnamon 3 cups (12 oz./340 g) pecan halves

Got a craving for something sweet, crunchy, and addictive? Look no further than these spiced pecans. Inspired by Mexican-churro flavors and Chinese candied walnuts, these spicy miso-glazed nuts are salty, sweet, and warming from the ginger and cayenne. They make a terrific snack on their own, or are the perfect crunchy topping for the Avocado Parfait with Coconut Miso Dressing. Try them in any application where you would traditionally use candied nuts: salads, sundaes, or as gifts for friends—the recipe is easily doubled or tripled. The nuts are best made fresh, although any leftovers can be stored at room temperature in an airtight container for up to three days.

CHAPTER 7

Beverage Fusion Innovations

It was a variation on a classic. Instead of the classic Vienna pure beef dog, smothered with mustard and raw onion, Knack wrapped a German wiener in a warmed poppy-seed bun, then enveloped it in a blend of beef chili and sliced onion. Today, many of the restaurants in the area claim ownership of the ultimate product, and each has its proponents. Each offers variations on the theme, including the trademarks of the original O'Doogies, a local favorite when nothing else could be settled in high school.

The average consumer may not ever serve a Twinkle to guests, but knowing what inspired the competition in the big bar in the sky is crucial to creating sophisticated signature beverages for your own audience. The invention of the 20th-century classic—the Skyline Coney Island—is credited to a proprietor of the once underprescribed hang-outs after hours near cities' transportation centers. With a microphone in front of him and in the midst of the broadcast invention brouhaha at the Chicago World's Fair, he concocted a new style of hot dog that was to find fame as a midnight snack.

7.1. Cocktail Fusion Trends

This is not really a new concept considering that historical cocktails are themselves an interesting fusion of indigenous ingredients combined with exotic spices and initial alcohols brought by Spanish, Portuguese, and British colonists. These pages want to give you an insight into some of the most interesting contemporary fusion trends that are emerging to drive our palates upon a journey of imagination and creativity.

One of the most contemporary movements in mixology today is the concept of uniting spirits, combining liquors, and cross-breeding flavors. New and even peculiar partnerships are emerging and cohabiting comfortably under the same glass. This indicates the high level of confidence of the current consumer who is willing to break the boundaries in which drinks had become encased.

7.2. Tea and Coffee Blends from Around the World

The special tastes that tea and coffee impart to foods without overwhelming their inherent natural flavors are part of the secret to creative cooking. The versatility and broad blend of pleasing flavors and aromas are utilized to add excitement to special dishes that touch the hearts and souls of the many tea and coffee connoisseurs. In the world of tea blends, Chai from the Indian subcontinent has made its inroad in several ethnic markets. In the world of coffee blends, some of the drinks associated with life, such as espresso, cappuccino, and a variety of iced coffee blends, have played an extensive role in the kitchens of the world, having found their place in many food dishes, drinks, salads, and even desserts. Try these special kitchen-tested blends of coffee and tea to delight friends and family members along with yourself.

Many cultures around the world have transformed the simple act of drinking tea or coffee into a moment of togetherness between friends or family, a sacramental experience, or a tradition that has to be followed several times throughout the day. Whether you start your day with a cappuccino and a cornetto, or with a cup of bitter and strong tea like the Russians, the custom of offering someone a drink is as wide and varied as the countries that the drinks represent. Tea and coffee are exotic, laden with tradition, and full of cultural and anthropological significance. These drinks have inspired the world's leading writers, and lately, they have found additional uses as they are utilized in creative cooking to complement flavors in sweet and savory dishes.

CHAPTER 8

Fusion Flavors for Special Diets

Dairy and vegetarian cuisine: Indian cuisine does not contain much cheese; people there get their calcium from the generous use of legumes and vegetables. However, ghee, a kind of clarified butter, is used to cook many of the dishes. Chinese cuisine can be an excellent partner to Indian cuisine for the vegetarian; both believe in quick-cooking vegetables lightly with a mixture of soy and ginger. With a few basic techniques from Chinese and the subtle Indian flavorings, you may never again consider it difficult to be "vegetarian."

Meat-eaters aren't the only ones who can enjoy the excitement of fusion cooking. In fact, vegetarian and vegan fusion dishes are some of the most popular offerings from restaurant kitchens today. Fusion cooking is generally low in animal fat, and when you're dealing with ingredients from two different regions, one tends to cancel out some of the possible dietary excesses of the other.

8.1. Vegan-Friendly Fusion Recipes

Vegans are also much more cognizant of healthful foods, so the flavors in their dishes have to be intense. Fusion cooking designed for vegans can enliven all of us to welcome more vegetables into our diets. Vegan fusion cooking uses every cultural method of developing flavor to create tasty dishes. They stuff flatbreads with Thai Red Lentil Spread and Fermented Coconut Chutney, or with Italian Eggplant Salad and go southeast. Refreshing vegan sides like Teeny Weeny Meyer Lemon Pickles or Quick-Pickled Mustard Seeds can accompany any fusion dish.

The current trend of eating vegan foods provides the perfect opportunity to embrace all the amazing flavors that come from cooking vegetables and fruits. Produce has its own special set of tasty attributes, which can be appreciated by the most discerning of diners, vegan or omni. Plus, with the large variety of flavor agents and ethnic seasonings available, it would take a lifetime to get through them all. Many ethnic cuisines are plant-based, and with a nudge from the cook, can be made vegan. Yet, other cuisines have a ready-for-vegan concept. So, there really is no lack of inspiration for creating an inspired, hyper-flavorful vegan meal.

8.2. Gluten-Free Fusion Options

1. Banh Mi Lettuce Wraps - A banh mi is basically a Vietnamese sandwich, so calling these lettuce wraps a banh mi might be a bit of a cheat. But you can include all the same toppings, minus the bread, and it's pretty spot-on! There really isn't a recipe for this, per se. All you need to do is cook up some pork, chicken, beef, or tofu, wrap it inside some lettuce leaves, and pile on all the banh mi fixins to your heart's content. If you'd like a little bit more of a structured meal idea, try one of these lettuce wrap options.

Gluten is found in wheat, rye, and barley, and for those with gluten sensitivities, discovering food they can eat can often be a struggle. By their nature, fusion foods incorporate multiple culinary traditions, so it's actually quite easy to come up with options that are already naturally gluten-free, like ceviche and fried rice. However, if you have a hankering for a specific kind of fusion recipe that does include gluten, you can choose to substitute. Go for a gluten-free soy sauce, use rice or corn-based noodles instead of wheat, or try almond, chickpea, tapioca, or coconut flour instead of the whole grain flours.

CHAPTER 9

Fusion Flavors for Entertaining

- Hazelnut vegetable dip: Forget the oniony, mayonnaisy, mix-stuff-in-a-box soup recipes from Midwestern Baptist hellscapes. Here's a vegetable dip that looks and tastes like its origins—Japan. Any sturdy vegetable, cracker, or chip pairs well with this umami-rich dip. At Ichimura in Manhattan, they serve vegetable tempura with anarachan dipping sauce; my version is in homage to that dish. Butter-steamed and a quick hazelnut-ify, the green vegetables turned into a harmonious mash and dance along the tiny flakes of the smashed nuts. They shimmy in concert, but each keeps their very own individual essence intact. The recipe is far from forgettable and it is quick and easy to make. "Hazelnut-yuzu froth," as an ingredient or finishing touch, is optional; but hazelnut-yuzu froth will lead to more/louder boisterous appetizer adulations.

Thanks to Daniel Boulud and Jean-Georges Vongerichten, among others, French and Japanese flavors have been entertaining together for years. Let's call them glamorously synched sidemates. Add a spoonful of Korean in the mix and the results are shamelessly delightful. When entertaining, less is often more, and I have designed a few dips, pickles, and savory small plates that greedily mix the flavors of Japan and the charms of Gallic complexity with a hip Korean twist. Serve them as a conglomerate of simple bites or swerve into a cohesive meal with a plated portion of Vietnamese-inspired beef-five spice demi-glace to gently nestle Gallic–Sichuan–Gallic heights.

9.1. Party Platter Ideas

Sometimes, a party platter can solve problems such as what to do with all the leftovers. When you find yourself with a bounty of salads, either of greens or composed, such as a variation of Caprese, or mixed diced vegetables, use the salad bases in an omelet or quesadilla, all of which can be presented at the table, doing double duty as a buffet of sorts. A virtual mash-up of some of the dishes presented here could all be prepared and served family style, making it easy for the hostess to quickly pull together a cocktail party on a moment's notice. Remember that vegetable platters or selections of olive concoctions, pickles, and nuts can all be used to cost effectively form the base of this sort of party. What's great about a party platter is that everything doesn't necessarily have to be made from scratch. Your guests will remember a fabulous platter the next morning, not how perfect your Caesar salad dressing was.

Whether it's a small group relegated to the sidelines to watch a sports event on a too-small television screen or a family gathered around the coffee table in the living room, everyone likes a party platter! A party platter is not so much a recipe as it is an "idea prompt" for the cook to be creative. Think of things such as tossing a company casserole on the cutting board into an omelet, a casserole pot pie topping, or burrito filling. Martha Stewart has even put party platters into her wedding menus using Caprese, Niçoise, and Salade Lyonnaise themes. Sometimes, there is no easier way of serving the old standby of "Fill Your Own Tacos" than setting up a taco bar on the counter and letting guests play with the fillings. Sometimes, a meal might be no more than some good bread, cold cuts, a few nice cheeses, pickles, and some bread condiments. It's no more work and always tastes so much better.

9.2. Brunch Fusion Delights

A serving can have 3 one-stick wedges, or have diners rip off waffle ball noshes. Serve warm and drizzle with honey, or serve warm with warm maple syrup. Alternatively, dip in honey mustard sauce. To reheat in the microwave, cover with a paper towel. Microwave on high for 15 to 20 seconds. Serves 10 to 12. The French term for a lemon slice with a zest ribbon is lemon wheel with a twist.

This dish utilizes cold wedge-shaped waffles to create a small finger food that looks like a yellow pool floatie. Please look at the ingredient picture to see how the kabob looks! Warm the back side of each waffle in a low oven (200°F) or in a microwave for a few seconds. Match waffles evenly into wedges so that the outside edge of one wedge faces the inside edge of the second wedge. Continue this action until 5 waffle completes are made. Press each pair of waffles so that they meld into one waffle. Trim each waffle to make a uniform look. The cool method would be safe for students to run bamboo skewers along the outer edge of one waffle and through to the outer edge of the connected waffle. Skewer pairs. Centers should face outward. On each pair, slide on the following ingredients: A baton of Canadian bacon that has been folded into a strip at the top, a caper berry, a lemon slice and caper berry, and a lemon slice; repeat sequence for each skewer.

- 10 waffle wedges, cooked - 10 fresh lemon slices - 10 large caper berries - 10 slices Canadian bacon

This might start out as a breakfast on a stick creation, but it also would be great for brunch, lunch, or just a fun appetizer or snack. It's simple, quick and the physical components cook at the same rate. It's like a strange kabob, but on a stick and a fun finger food. This dish can also be finished as a sweet or savory version with warm maple syrup or a warm honey mustard sauce. Prep time for culinary students is 20 minutes as the melding waffles are cooking; actual prep time is about 10 minutes. On a consumer or home cook level, especially utilizing a microwave, the recipe would be an easy fix and the prep time would be less than 10 minutes.

CHAPTER 10

Conclusion: Embracing Creativity in the Kitchen

If you think of your meals as being a new creation with each garnish, you're guaranteed to combat the lure of fast food and convenience meals. The strides we've made in recent years have made it easier than ever to cook from scratch in even the busiest kitchen, utilizing technology and convenience cooking methods to make meals that were once labor-intensive into completely manageable tasks. Making a Beef and Pinto Bean Stew could take all day, but now you can make it quickly with the aid of your panini grill. Take a spin through the ingredient list, the main idea will emerge quite easily. The end result, even if different from stew, will be a quick and tasty supper using a large number of the tastes and textures of the original dish. By the end of the recipe, you'll understand how to balance the beef and pinto beans with a highly flavored broth.

Learning to think creatively about cooking is one of the most valuable skills you can acquire, and discovering the brilliance of great world cuisines. It will give rise to the question "What's for dinner tonight?" Whether you're feeding yourself, your family, or a party of friends, this new way of approaching food is truly an inspiration. Instead of always relying on the tried and true (yet probably tired) recipes you've been making for years, why not bring some new ideas to the table? One way to do that is to use this book as a springboard to ignite your creativity. The techniques and recipes we've provided are only a starting point from which to let your imagination soar. As you browse through the food chapters, consider the flavors you really enjoy and don't be afraid to mix and match your favorites to create dishes that truly represent your personal style.

Milton Keynes UK
Ingram Content Group UK Ltd.
UKHW040329031224
452051UK00011B/313

9 798330 600687